The Swing at the Edge of the World

poems by

Lea Graham

Finishing Line Press
Georgetown, Kentucky

The Swing at the Edge of the World

ACKNOWLEDGMENTS

"Red Fox Sighting: 9 A.M., London's East End" published in *I-70 Review*
"When You're in Romania & Wish You Were Alone" was published in
    Gargoyle #70
"On the Ionian" was published in *Typishly*
"In a Polish Dream" won the Michelle Boisseau Poetry Prize in 2022 and was
    published in *Bear Review*
"Why Don't We All Stay Home" published in *Kestrel*
"It Seems the Whole World Has Forgotten Us," and "Love's Travel Stop" and
"For Breedlove, in Spain," "For Wayne Zade..." and "Starting with a Line
    from Pasolini" in *Valley Voices*

Publisher: Leah Huete de Maines
Editor: Christen Kincaid
Cover Art: Yoav Horesh
Author Photo: Lea Graham
Cover Design: Elizabeth Maines McCleavy

Order online: www.finishinglinepress.com
also available on amazon.com

Author inquiries and mail orders:
Finishing Line Press
PO Box 1626
Georgetown, Kentucky 40324
USA

Contents

For Mark—
a garden, a store house, a party, a multitude of counselors

*"The only geography
we have is the storybooks of our childhood."*
—Jack Gilbert *"Eating with the Emperor"*

*"To create time
Relinquish space—that is, the place
Where the time used to be."*
—Kenneth Koch *"On Aesthetics"*

When You're in Romania & Wish You Were Alone

      with these donkeys clacking down the streets
of Brașov, leading their cows to milking,
with pastries you can't pronounce & bottles
of Ursus or Ciuc chugged
on a standing-room-only bus,
Queen Marie's castle towers above
(known as "Vlad's place"), her heart
stolen away, hidden nearby
in nested boxes from the Nazis
or because of her love of this country...
this country where you came
for a little Carpathian
silence, to watch over the garlic,
lie on St. Andrew's stone bed,
to light candles for guidance.

Instead, you're trapped as he smokes
& tosses butts outside
the airport, no help
deciphering the taxi racket,
he lounges against a wall as if
it's some bar in Beantown between
jam sessions. The ride, reckless & blurred,
past strip clubs & paneláks
to the tourist section
with this rock & roll loser
who knows every score to every game
down to cricket but can't pick up
the tab for anything except
the one ticket it took to get him
here & here you are in a whirl
of Romanian (closest
to Old Latin, you once read)
& his complaints, stacking up
even faster before it's over

until you find yourself underneath
a hotel in a room pounding
karaoke in Arabic,
Spanish, German, English,
a glow-in-the-dark mini-golf course—

Red Fox Sighting: 9 A.M., London's East End

How small & openly furtive
they are, "as numerous as pubs here."

There's still *Fish & Chips*
& fog around each corner.

Maybe just a false memory
from the Sherlock black & whites

I used to watch in that house
on Unicorn Road. Remember?

Lying on the couch for days
with the dog. Silent, the ex would come in,

look at the prone body fixed
on the next episode with secret letters,

the sound of rain, a slow suspense of deduction—
Where do we go when there's no place to go?

The fox & I retreat into a fiction
of landscape: trot through streets,

search out the scraps behind the stoop.

It Seems the Whole World Has Forgotten Us

to Celia Bland

is what she said
that morning
in the field
after coffee & larvae,
tortilla & beans,
after night's
isolate chill,
sheets spread
on the ground
in this camp
somewhere north
of Tapachula.

This woman from Quiché,
living a few *milpas*
away from her own
country for ten years.

The dew blinked
from stalks, small boys
took their morning piss
in the river
& we all wanted
to cry at these words,
but understood
the luxury—

& so I cry
extravagantly
each time & now
here with my friend
when I tell this story
already 25 years old.

For Breedlove, in Spain

> *There's nothing worse*
> *than feeling bad and not*
> *being able to tell you.*
> *—Frank O'Hara, "Nocturne"*

In Rosendale, NY
when your laughter is better
to me than most things
& counterpoised to the light
of San Sebastián where
you should have been
looking up circumspect
from your book
& pinxto of sardine
with olives without
amazement at
the rain about to
come or end.

You are often in Spain
with me, remember?
The Boss playing
Santiago—that ancient field
of spontaneous combustion
where you swore to ride
your scooter from Toulouse.
I was a mess then.
Crying into my café con leche
at any old pop song
and a message one morning
from Betsy Huang that Tapply
had died, Hemingway's
own doppelganger, who cheered
me on to the pain of a new life.

But listen:
a bus took me off
into the end
of the world where Romans
believed ghosts roamed
the sightline, where I found
my own German shoemaker.
We burned maps
& socks in
the pocks of a cliff.

Anything *might could* change.

In A Polish Dream

I am sleeping & driving
from the back seat
through night & snow.

Waking, still in the dream,
I realize & reach for the wheel.
Something isn't right about my life.
I am excited
driving this dark away
from the past into
other pasts.

Years later & one morning,
our Polish neighbors across the way
have given us pork & bread
spread with lard for breakfast.

The night before, you sang
"Happy Birthday" with a woman
named Beata, drank vodka
& wine in a rectangle of light,
raised our glasses
with these unknown,
familiar people
here on the Adriatic coast,
near Dante's grave.

What We Can't Get Away From

"Hotel California" playing p.a.'s from Kota Kinabalu hotels to Atacames, the buskers of Galway, that Sofia hair salon.

Michael Jackson & Elvis & The Beatles on that bus through Mexico City or in the streets of Cali waiting & watching the one-legged pigeons, men playing checkers as we washed our hands in coffee.

U.S. sitcoms & cop shows: Seinfeld in Croatia, *How I Met Your Mother* from Edinburgh to Orkney, *T.J. Hooker* in Hungary, the dubbed *Law & Order SVU* in Paris that sleepless night
without darkness.

Feral dogs looping beaches on the Black Sea, running Conway's alleys, friendlier near Tanji & Samaná, hangdog-sad or left to die in Baños.

Immigration forms that never allow answers for the questions posed—

Cinderblock from Dakar to Joal, the classrooms of Les Cayes, among wood smoke in Atitlán, the Sunday schools of Figure Five, Stuttgart, Lavaca; that first room on the Cuyabeno before fishing piranhas, chopping snakeheads, searching waters for the pink dolphin.

Statues of men at war on horseback: Lafayette, Buenos Aires, Capitoline Hill in hats or without, with swords or guns or spears, sometimes cannons.

Coca-Cola & crows & the mosquitos of Mombasa, Río Dulce, here in Florence, yonder in Snowball.

The self, the self, the self.

When You're in Kota Belud at Ramadan & the Only Thing Open Is KFC

Here, rice has replaced biscuits, but the three-piece extra-crispy is the
    same.
Two little boys compare their bright flip-flops & mothers pick quietly
at their slaw or lean to babies in their pastel hijabs & abayas, the
golden spire of the mosque down the street pierces blue like steeples
in any old town & Mount Kota Kinabalu poses, a beautiful idea.

We have not seen pygmy elephants nor the *Wild Man of Borneo*. We
have floated among lightning bugs like tacky Christmas lights along
the Kiulu river, watched Korean teens do herkies on the beach near
herds of cows. But the *Finger-lickin' Good* above this stainless-steel
counter—that's just obscene.

Senegambia Beach Hotel, October 20, 2016

Turkey buzzards breakfast
on a white rat

A monitor lizard
lives near the drain pipe

Here, we are called "America"

The ATM's give only 3000 Dalasis
at once but charge 200 each time

The hibiscus are small
but salmon-colored, perfect

The BBC tells us that Obama has called
Trump "a whiner"

(& he is so cool saying it that
we are in love all over again)

The Philippines plans to chemically
castrate sex offenders

Each time they interview Duterte
his face smiles gently as the waters of El Nido

In Romania there is a refuge
for dancing bears

In the middle of each night
I wake just a bit

my arm on your chest
or your arm over my shoulder—

I want to say "cradling" me, but
more in the shape of a gaff—gaffing me with love

& I think in that moment
how happy in the moment

& each night I am with you
& how even happier I am

in knowing how happy
I am with you

You have seen colonus monkeys
each morning & I have seen

dolphins on the ferry from Banjul
to Barra before Jaffureh

before Kunta Kinte Island
formerly known as James Island

& before that St. Andrew
by the Portuguese

The gray monkeys we have no name
for eat sugar cubes,

Domoda is the peanut sauce
so heavy & comforting & light

Solomon has guided us,
Aisa painted my toenails *Madeira Wine*

We have smoked with Junior & Faburama
under the Freedom Tree

Musa served us gin
& tonics & pizza & lady fish yassa,

Ellen has cleaned our room each day—her name is
my great-grandmother's, my own name.

I wore my sunglasses on the island
when Doudou spoke of slavery

those 15 million kidnappings
How do we not know all of this?

Florence Morning

Where I wake from a dream
to the bells & mosquitos
in November. The light is always
an idea. Today we will board
a train that runs a length
of this country, these kingdoms.
I say: *Lecce* then *Galipoli* over &
over. It tastes like *here*.
Sometimes place is familiar,
but not because it's known.
Somehow in strangeness
it is gentler, a privacy

On the Ionian

There was a trumpet
player outside the hotel window playing
"The Lambada." Two boys pushed a wheel-
chair behind him loaded with tools:
hammer, wrenches, step-ladder.
The last time I heard that song
maybe fifteen years ago outside
a bar, Boca Chica, another world.

Now outside this trattoria
with a plate of orecchiette—*little ears*
& the house white, a color of January sun.
It is December here near the *see-through sea.*
Gallipoli. Puglia. Where names send me.

The Greek fountain in this piazza
so eroded no faces nor defined
limbs can be seen—only gestures:
one figure plucking something
above him; another leans slightly
left as if to dodge a small rock,
a bad word. These reclining ladies
seem more at the beach than in bed.
White conical adornments make
a cut-out of the sky that poses
like an ad for pleasure or something
ancient, a nicer name for *old.* I marvel
that the past had no word for *blue.*

In my mind, alone & not alone,
the worries & wishes &
angers & words of others
comment on this moment.
The trumpet player is off playing
a song where someone is turning
on a dance floor, where the frill
of a skirt makes the difference,

a song in which I have spent a
secretive hour as if slipping
outside this world unnoticed.
His sons are skipping rocks into
this bay or unfolding the ladder or
practicing at wrench & hammer.

Gulls fly across this plastic
tablecloth, a small roar of Vespas,
real gulls above the castle & flag,
giant bowls of *vongole rosso*
& cozze for sale in the market,
a bridge named *John Paul II*,
each time someone passes:
buon giorno—good day, good journey.

Small monuments of a small moment
when I did not want to change my life.

Scotland Sentences

The love can always outweigh the grief
—Cheryl Strayed

In which I walked the Great Glenn Way,
learned the last wolf was spotted in 1971.

A poet & his wife took me in during those days
in Drumnadrochit, the Loch Ness Monster

Museum just down the road & their sign
on the door: *Quiet. American Poet Sleeping.*

Grieved against a castle wall in Fort William,
my legs rubber in Inverness after sheep & oranges,

a stint of tundra. I couldn't get enough wine.
Ran into trouble at a cèilidh with a tattooed man,

found kin in the museum: those broad faces familiar
through generations. I've never been so lonesome.

Only the mother & her young sons just back
from training began the mend

when she gave me a ride (my first hitchhike!)
asked if I was *an axe murderer?*

An off-the-grid Welshman on the ferry to Orkney:
drank pints, deciphered accents,

our goodbye remains.
The Surgeons' Museum with its notebooks

of human skin, its balls & chains
of war—where I learned how we

learned to heal
through pain, destruction.

It rained some & I watched *How I Met Your Mother*—
the ASL interpreter looked like Uncle Bill.

When I think of this now, here
from a window looking south to Santa Maria del Fiore,

there is a transom of blue among clouds
& days stretch before me

Fort Ozama Engagement

March 20, 2016

Where you tell me I wear your *heart*
on my finger & we lean
between battlements looking down
at the Ozama with its tankers
in dock, out to that otherworldly blue
that is the Caribbean & this morning

I learn that this fort was built
by African & Taino slaves
with coral, cemented
in lime & bulls' blood,
making it more
impenetrable with years.

It is hard to escape
the heft of the metaphor
of lives built on the backs
of others, materials we have stolen,
constructed vantage points
to defend ourselves, survive attacks—

To keep living makes a courage

For Wayne Zade, After the Death of a Poet, January 14, 2016

Upon reading the news
this morning I think: Paris!
Could we escape the impending
not here there among the light
& spires or in some louche corner
of Shakespeare & Co., where my husband
once lived, telling me stories of butter-eating
George with his fire-singed hair
in the final days, dying upstairs while
the Scottish daughter scowled at
the register as she banned any hope of return.

Everything these days seems
aimed at or thumbing heaven—
another destination on no one's
bucket list but a place we're all bound.

Yet, I'm sitting here now
drinking pretty good coffee, thinking
about you & the way you tell stories
about other poets in that intimate,
ironic way & your enduring
love for music & language & students—
enthusiams!—*en theos!*
& the sun is on the avenue
& Komunyakaa is on the docket
& there's a salsa station even here
in Conway, Arkansas.

Love's Travel Stop

        what we pass on our way
towards the Hernando De Soto
Bridge just off I-40 north of Palestine
where you talk rice and goldfish
grown in those fallow fields where
51% of the world's carnival prizes
are raised, where you name Stuttgart:
World's Best Duck Hunting.

Names & where they send a mind—
"The Swing at the Edge of the World"
where I swung out over Tungurahua's
black-green ravines, under the skies of Los Baños,
or Jerusalem last December
where t-shirts declared *Guns & Moses*
en route to Masada then the Dead Sea
where I floated at the lowest point on earth.
Where I was then. That blue, unearthly, amniotic.

These things & places transform place.
Here is stranger this time. A doubleness. Polysemy?
Etymology? How we say *in the past*....
another geography we drive through
on the way to the *Home of the Blues*

Starting with a Line from Pasolini

Draws on "The Song of the Bells" from Pier Paolo Pasolini's
Roman Poems, trans. Lawrence Ferlinghetti & Francesca
Valente, 2005

When evening loses itself in the fountains

I am congratulated with the yellow lights

from corner shops, the *Four Seasons*

of Santa Trinitá, once decapitated

and fished from the Arno after the war.

Everyone is far away & this bridge

crowded with lovers, cameras, canes tapping

stone & fissure; alive in the wheeling

murmurations & bell song.

There is no village waiting,

no love returns me from this distance.

Why Don't We All Stay Home

Until a few years ago,
half of Columbus's corpse
was lying in Sevilla,
the other half in Santo Domingo.

Do you bury a conqueror
in the land he conquered or
the land for which he conquered?
Is travel within or outside of us?

It's hard to get away.
That significant apple
near the Rias Baixas;
Julbrews under the Freedom Tree.

The three Dubliners who hitchhiked
from Tel Aviv to Galway
(just to meet me); the Romanian
kid with his blackberry juice
an afternoon in Cali.

Bodies in place; bodies that place.
"Travel" rooted in *travail*;
yet, we insist *revel*.
Years ago, I read the story

of two Cameroonian brothers
who stowed away in the boiler room
of *Atlas*, an ocean liner
headed for Marseilles. Burning by noon,

cold all night, they dreamt of boredom,
of waking to the same dirt alley
with the same old roosters & rice
& the women singing down the day.

Lea Graham is a writer, editor, critic and translator who lives in Hyde Park, New York. She has traveled to over 40 countries and lived in Florence, Italy; Quito, Ecuador and Santiago, Dominican Republic. She is the author of three poetry collections, *The O.E.D. Odes* (MadHat Press, 2026), *From the Hotel Vernon* (Salmon Press, 2019) and *Hough & Helix & Where & Here & You, You, You* (No Tell Books, 2011), along with a fine press book and three chapbooks.

She is the co-editor with Celia Bland of *A Jar of Air: The Work of Maxine Chernoff* (MadHat Press 2026) and the editor of *From the Word to the Place: The Work of Michael Anania* (MadHat Press, 2022). She is associate professor of English at Marist College in Poughkeepsie, NY and a native of Northwest Arkansas.